CÔTE d'AZUR

THE FRENCH RIVIERA

CÔTE d'AZUR

THE FRENCH RIVIERA

Text by Jacques Robichon
Translated by Don Monson

"Azure Coast" is the French name for the French Riviera. Azure: blue (as the atmosphere, the waves, etc.) derived from Latin *azzurum* which comes from the Arab *al-azurd*, the blue, and from the Arabo-Persian *lazuverd*, lapis lazuli, the famous "azure stone." Coast: line of contact between the dry land and the sea, shore, seaboard.

But here it's the sky—and nearly it alone—which is blue: not the shore, not the coastline which, rock, sand, gravel and pebbles, steep or gently sloping as it enters the water, takes most of its colors from its basic contour and from the immediate environment: blood from the red rocks rolling verdant crests between the deep azure of the waters and the paler, markedly less intense azure of the sky, to which the sea jealously poses as a faithful, reflecting and vibrant mirror in the implacable seething of the sun-king.

The name itself, one of the most famous in the world, who gave it to it? From whom did the "Azure Coast", maritime balcony of the Provençal country, get its name? And when? It is generally agreed that the official act of baptism of the French "Riviera" goes back to the end of the nineteenth century and that it can even be assigned a date supported by unempeachable bibliographical references: 1887.

That year, Mr. Stephen Liégeard, French writer, poet, essayist and novelist, who had been a Deputy during the Second Empire and hardly suspected that he would one day become the grandfather of a heroic grandson named Georges Guynemer, became famous by publishing a work devoted to that region of the Mediterranean shores which he esteemed above all else. The book was honored by the French Academy, which did not suspect at all, however, what reverberations awaited its title. Liégeard had called it: *La Côte d'Azur*.

Historically, the "Azure Coast" has existed less than one hundred years, is not yet a centenarian. Geographically, what are its extent and its limits? The "Azure Coast," invented for touristic purposes, is neither a province (like Burgundy, Normandy, Brittany or Alsace) nor even a department

3 Cultivation of carnations above Cape Ferrat.

←————————————

1 Nice. Baie des Anges.

2 Juan-les-Pins.

(like Corsica), although it stretches across several. Where does the "Azure Coast" begin and end? That is the double, supreme and inevitable question; also the touchiest, giving rise to disputes and controversies.

Where it ends we know: at the ravine of the Saint-Louis Brook in the outskirts of Menton, right at the gates of Italy, continued by the Ligurian pomp of the *Riviera dei fiori*, the Riviera of Flowers. The difficulty arises as soon as one tries to determine with a minimum of probable certainty where to the west, sixty miles (100 km) or more away, the traveler has crossed the frontiers of the enchanted country.

The opinions are many and, on that account, violently opposed, often irreconcilable to the point of extreme vehemence. It is well known, for example, that the great majority of Provençal people starting twenty-five or thirty miles (40-50 km) inland, proud - legitimately - to be what they are and can't help being, are easily credited with forcefully challenging and repudiating, if not abominating, the coastal fringe of their native province between Marseilles and Ventimiglia. "The sea, that horrible sandpaper which wears down rocks, bodies and souls...," in the words of Giono, who could never pardon the Provençal coast "its miles of naked women hung out to dry," adding, "I have noticed that there are fewer imbeciles at an altitude of ten thousand feet (3,000 m) than at sea-level." But Giono is, fundamentally, unshakeably, a sedentary landlubber with highlander tendencies. Besides, the Mediterranean always interested him less than the Atlantic or the English Channel; to ask him to sing the praises of its marvels, its paradise, is out of the question.

However, the anathema flung from Manosque didn't resolve, for all that, the essential question, which remains in doubt: where should we place the entrance gate to that Gold-and-Azure Coast so steadfastly contested, simultaneously Provençal and Mediterranean. Alain Decaux, historiographer of its "Brilliant Moments" as well as fervent enthusiast of its contemporary charms, didn't hesitate to follow Stephen Liégeard in placing the beginning of the French Riviera at the legendary palm-lined avenues of Hyères, in the Var, the greatest concentration per square mile of these monocotyledonous plants since the outskirts of Marseilles.

For her part, the Provençal woman Marie Mauron, from Baux, displays more impetuosity in assigning Toulon as the starting point. But in that case, why

4 Marseilles. Our Lady of La Garde and the Old Port.

5-6-7 Marseilles. The Old Port - Rue Longue-des-Capucins - The Vallon des Auffes.

8-9-10 Calanque of Port-Miou - Cassis - The Château d'If.
11 Calanque near Cassis.

12 *Les Lecques.*

13 *Sanary.*

14 *La Ciotat.*

15 *Bandol.* "*The improvisor.*"

16 *The Gros-Cerveau road.*

17 *Saint-Maximin-la-Sainte-Baume.*

18. *Toulon.   The market of the Cours Lafayette.*

not Le Brusc, Sanary or Bandol? Why not La Ciotat and Cassis? Others opt more obviously in favor of Le Lavandou, in line with Cape Bénat; others, still more radical, obliterating quite frankly the nearness of the mosaic of the three golden isles, Porquerolles, Port-Cros and Le Levant, don't hesitate to name Saint-Tropez — taking simultaneously into account arguments from the surrounding snobism, from vogue and fashion and from the rudiments of an elementary geography.

But others, the overwhelming majority, feel that they must conform to a more accurate appraisal of historical fact, combined with that of a certain tradition, if not of the decor itself and of the geology, by restrictively limiting the territory of the French Riviera, the enchanted kingdom, to that distance alone, reduced to sixty-five miles (104 km), which separates Saint-Raphaël from Menton. And after all, they are probably right.

Shall I admit that, as far as I am concerned, the French Riviera begins at the Château d'If in the Bouches-du-Rhône, at the foot of the rock of La Garde Hill, continues all the way to the little bay of Saint-Cyr in the Var, and finally penetrates, through capes, promontories, corniches, valleys and forests, into the Alpes-Maritimes, to the heart of the Esterel, among the red porphyry rocks of Miramar, thus covering three departments and including the whole of the Provençal coast—or about one hundred forty-five miles (230 km)—, from Marseilles to the Italian frontier?
Indeed, is it right to include in the royalty of this Coast of the Sun only the specific landscapes and settings of its most famous and prestigeous area, of its most privileged sphere? Is it fair to exclude the whole length of the Marseilles coast, plus the Toulon coast, as well as the homeland of Maurin des Maures, in other words—except for a small fringe of about twenty miles (30 km)—the entire coast of the Var? I certainly do not think so.

Coastal Lower Provence with its plateaus of blue rock, crossed by "garrigues" or wastelands with rough and dusty roads, among the abandoned sheep-folds or ancient, solitary farms at the edge of woods of quivering olive-trees, in the clamour of frenetic colonies of cicadas; rock and limestone of the seafront, peaks, saw-tooth ridges, faults and high, chalky gorges where, at the farthest ledge of a sheer cliff, a clump of Aleppo pines hangs its royal crown; brutal indentations in the shoreline, coves with chaotic walls and great, vertiginous "calanques" (deep coves) in the hills of Marseilleveyre and of Cassis, last vestiges of those submerged valleys cut out by colossal rapier-thrusts and as if suspended above the scintillating abyss of the sea; from the Bec de l'Aigle (Eagle's Beak) of La Ciotat to the peninsula of Sicié, forest-covered, abrupt, wild, then from the roasdstead of

Toulon, defended by its cirque of haughty summits, all the way to the Gulf of Giens southernmost projection of the Provençal coast; from the plain of Hyères to the beginning of the Maures Corniche with its dazzling foliage of rose-laurels overhanging the whirl-wind development of the shore; finally, from the Ramatuelle Massif to the five fierce capes of the peninsula of Saint-Tropez, and from the coast of Sainte-Maxime to the mouth of the Argens, facing the belltowers, domes, ornamental facades, palm-lined boulevards and gardens of the white city of Saint-Raphaël, inserted between the green of the hills, the blue of the water and the red of the rock sculpted by the seawind... Each of the segments of this amazing longitudinal puzzle, taken separately or placed end-to-end, constitues so many stages to be passed through, gradations, transitory thresholds, so many intermediate landings and—if one may say so—brilliant antechambers in the distribution and subtle progression of the coast of Profence, before reaching the heart of the royal country.

*
* *

A rather good way to discover a region or a country is to catch it from above, that is, from the summits. The coast of the Var offers such an opportunity on at least two occasions, the first right in the outskirts of Toulon.

Leaving the town of Six-Fours at sea-level, the road branches off, rises little by little through the heavy massif covered with oaks and pines of the Janas Forest, and climbs to its final crest (1,211 feet - 369 meters): the sharp rock of the Mount of the May-Tree. Up to there, nothing which is not very normal and usual: The winding roads of Janas distill their pungent, full-bodied aromas, distribute their light and shade. Suddenly, at the very edge of a crag, near the remains of a former watch-tower from the sixteenth century, straight up above the mighty promontory of Cape Sicié, the image freezes on one of the most grandiose panoramas of the Provençal coast.

Behind, Toulon and its high guard of blue mountains, the tall, modern buildings, the basins and their quays, the port traffic. Ahead, the sea horizon, the Mediterranean, slack, sumptuous, immense. On a day when the Mistral is blowing, that erratic wind which sweeps away all impurity, which corrodes and sharpens everything like the steel of an etching, the view is then stupendous: to the west the unfolding of the whole jagged coastal zone and its hinterland, from the Embiez Archipelago all the way to the islands of Marseilles, and to the east the marvelous, fantastic and joyous pageant of the shore pounded by the waves, from the green bursts of Toulon's Outer

**19-20-21 Toulon. The naval port - Quai Stalingrad -
The roadstead seen from Mount Faron.**

Roadstead along the Mourillon Corniche and from Cape Brun to the steep terraces of the Colle-Noire (Black Hill), to Carqueiranne, to l'Almanarre, to the Pesquiers Salt Marshes and to the first hills of the Maures, all the way to Giens, to the dazzling fleeciness of the Hyères Islands, separated from the rest, rising up from the deep, intense azure of the waves. In an instant, almost at a single glance, all is delivered; all is embraced, captured, fixed; all is said. "And the rest is silence."

The experience can be opportunely renewed about twenty-five miles (40 km) from there, at the crest — and at the heart — of another, equally climatic massif, which likewise juts out as glorious promontory above the Mediterranean, about halfway between Calvaire and Saint-Maxime. It is accessible from a small Provençal town, ancient, strange and thrice legendary: because its population pushed back the Sarrasins by casting furious swarms of bees upon the assailants, because a big elm-tree, planted in a small square, survies there from the time of Sully, and because at dusk one autumn evening in 1959, it received the remains of a young man of epic stature named Gérard Philipe. The town is Ramatuelle.

There, throughout centuries of insecurity, as in numerous other regions of Provence, the external walls of dwellings erected along the hill-side served themselves as their own walls of defense against foreign incursions, above the vast Pampelonne Plain, which was cultivated and coveted.

Soon the crests of the forest-covered hill raise up their first ruined edifices: one, then two, then a third. Neither towers nor look-outs, nor abandoned peasant huts, nor hunting blinds, nor fortified dwellings, but peaceful machines for grinding the grain of the fertile plain, at the spot on the hill where the winds come together best: these are the windmills of Paillas.

The fourth edifice, situated at the highest point (1,070 feet - 325 m) of the Saint-Tropez Peninsula, delivers the sight which we have come looking for, and first of all, straight ahead, the brilliant, promised sea washing the three miles (5 km) of fine sand of the wide Pampelonne Strand. Next, in a circular arc, from west to east, Cavalaire bay and, one by one, all the capes of the massive peninsula curving back into the gulf of Grimaud; the Sainte-Maxime coast continuing from there, with the wooded crests and ridges of the Maures remarkably close and distinct; then, emerging in the distance, the fantastic pile of reddish rocks and craggy peaks of the Esterel; then back to the horizon, which intersects the coastal summits at the level of Ventimiglia. Finally, to the north-east, way back, the Alps.

Here, too, in the light breeze bearing the subtle perfumes of that Mediterranean land forever unlike any other, the eye has instantly grasped everything, simultaneously recorded everything: the immense panorama of the sea, different and changing according to the seasons and the hours of the day, the intensity of the sun and the variation of the winds; the sky, whose colorations also rectify themselves imperceptibly according to the same meteorological laws; the landscape scenes in infinitely slow-motion, where wildness alter - nates with a strange and disconcerting gentleness, all of them alike, whether near or far, dependent at one time or another on the primacy of the Mediterranean.

*
* *

The two major poles, the determining factors in the attraction exerted by the French Riviera (in its whole or partial extension) are, as might be expected, the sun and then the sea: sovereign perenniality of the one's reign, permanence (or relative permanence) of the other's empire. Azure and gold.

It seems almost inconceivable that the French Riviera, which had received its letters patent, if not its nobility, before 1890, did not welcome its first summer visitors — the *estivants* — until a good forty years later,about 1925-1930. Nevertheless, the fact is there, irrefutable: up to the end of World War I, the Mediterranean part of southern France was really sought out, appreciated, esteemed by only a few of the very privileged, and only during a relatively limited season stretching from early winter to mid-spring.

From the onset of summer to the end of autumn, during which it rains frequently and unexpectedly, the marvelous "dream coast" harbored only its peaceful, hard-working native population, the only witnesses—or nearly so—to the fury of the July and August sun and to the sudden, absolutely torrential storms from October to December.

The great, terribly sun-drenched days of summer actively frightened away resort enthousiasts and, to tell the truth, put them to flight. Then the noble exodus poured, preferably, onto the beaches of the North Sea and the English Channel, from Ostend to Deauville. Who, indeed, would have had the (preposterous) idea of rushing, at that very time of year, to those Mediterranean shores celebrated by the justificatory lyricism of Stephen Liégeard, in order to undergo the onslaught of insane temperatures, the Saharan furnace, the wounds of a murderous sun, except of course, as a corollary to the climatic conditions, in order to throw off all one's clothes, or

22 *Fishermen near the Hyères Islands.*
23 *Porquerolles.*
24 *Cove on Port-Cros.*
25 *Porquerolles. The Plage d'Argent.*

30 *Brégançon Fort.*
31 *Le Lavandou.*
32-33 *Bormes-les-Mimosas.*

34-35 Saint-Tropez.

nearly so, and engage in the related activities suggested by the nearness of the sea, the sand and the rocks.

Exposure to the sun, baring the body to the full heat of the summer, was, in any case, still strictly unthinkable; its mere suggestion was the equivalent of a formal certification of delirium. The first concern of women, according to the canons of beauty then in force and to a long enduring fashion, was to acquire and keep a lilly-white complexion, an alabaster skin; and, consequently, to protect themselves very vigorously against any influence capable of upsetting such a steadfast purpose... To get a sunburn, that robust, hearty tan which would constitute the unanimous goal of vacationing generations to come: Fie! How vulgar! Leave that to the peasants!

So, for a long time, the Riviera coasts were frequented exclusively in winter, up to the first signs of spring: the marvelous audacity of Provence nature, favored by the presence of the Mediterranean and of exceptional temperatures, glorious blossoming of precocious plants, the sprouting of the first buds and the bursting forth of the young shoots, the fragrant breath of the orchards at noon, all of which giving way almost immediately to an explosion of plant-life in all directions.

Furthermore, visits to the region proved, in many ways, about as limited in space as in time: to the crowded winter season on the Blissful Coast, the strict equivalent was a vacation area which, except for a few resort islands scattered about in the Hyères region and around Saint-Tropez, stretched between the limits of Saint-Raphaël and Cannes, then from Nice to Menton. For a long time, for several generations of pioneers and adepts of Mediterranean travel, the enormous force of attraction of the French Riviera lay in the particular mildness of a privileged climate throughout those winter months when, at other latitudes of the Continent, reigned the deadly, interminable, completely disheartening gloomy season.

The sun, object of phobia and fear for the generation of the grandparents of those who now engage frenetically in the same place in systematic scorching, is not the exclusive privilege of the French Riviera, on the coast from Port-Vendres to Menton. But, statistically, it shines there about 320 days a year, which is a respectable record. On the other hand, it isn't perfectly constant, even during the season when it is customarily counted on the most: only July is assured of its almost total permanence; August and September prove to be more variable, less systematically favored, and June is not always more favored than they. In short, the *burning summer*, the "season of fire," hardly goes beyond a period equivalent to a little more than thirty dog days, which is relatively little.

It was long thought that the Mediterranean sun was a supreme remedy for curing tuberculosis and treating pulmonary lesions: it was a deadly error. And the fatal illusion continued for almost one hundred fifty years, right to the beginning of this century. The beautiful and passionate Marie Bashkirtseff came to Nice for the first time at the age of twelve; it was there that in 1882 she learned of the illness from which she would never recover; two years later she died of consumption, just short of her twenty-fourth birthday.

The sea itself, forever beginning anew, luminous, fascinating, contributed greatly to maintaining the illusion of a universal panacea: often asleep, barely crested with foam, with its shades of blue: cobalt, indigo, turquoise, metallic, cerulean... The Mediterranean does not, properly speaking, have tides: eight inches (20 cm) at Marseilles, an average of ten inches (25 cm) for the whole length of its coast (compared with thirty to fifty feet — 10-15 m — for the Atlantic Ocean and the English Channel). In speaking of sea-level, it's the Mediterranean which serves as a base, at least in France, for calculating various altitudes: absolute zero.

Below this level, an almost constant bottom line of about 330 feet (100 m) very close to the shore, from 1,300-1,700 feet (400-500 m) to about one-half mile (less than a kilometer) out. And although the short Mediterranean waves, with their rapid, compact motion, often make navigation difficult in bad weather, the swell of the waves on the Riviera proves in fact to be of small magnitude, low barometric pressures being rather rare outside of a few winter months.

The temperatures? It is important to state them with some objectivity: they are no longer what they were. The earth's crust is cooling, in southern France as elsewhere. The old residential villas of 1925, almost completely lacking in any coherent heating system, are now scarcely habitable from October or November on; in the last twenty years hotel establishments designed for winter vacationing have had to substantially overhaul their installations in order to withstand the combined onslaught of the humidity and the winds.

Comparatively speaking, it rains more today on the Mediterranean coast, and the cold proves more severe and more steadily persistent than thirty or

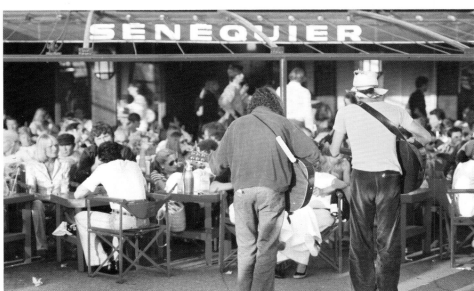

36 to 41 Saint-Tropez.
The quays.
A sidewalk café.
Boules players.
The marina.
Tahiti Beach.
Bay of Les Canebiers.

forty years ago. The Nice Carnival and the great battles of flowers, in February, are not always assured of taking place in absolutely splendid weather. The terrible winter of 1955 saw olive-trees die by the thousands right to the edge of the shores: throughout entire fields they raised up their trunks, blackened by the intense cold, in the face of the deadly-still sky; barely opened, the crystal flowers of the almond-trees, seared with frost, had disintegrated at the mere contact with the air. And then one morning, the winter wind died down, the sun blazed, setting aglow the country-side and the petrified coast; the incredible vivacity of the sap triumphed over the deadly abandonment of the wasted earth and began again to perform its age-old labor. The Mediterranean shores became once more the Frence Riviera.

That hadn't happened for seventy or eighty years. But such rigor remains exceptional for the season which formerly sealed the fame of the Mediterra-nean country. Although the temperatures of the Provençal coast have dropped considerably since 1930, they remain privileged and enviable at a time of year when fog, snow and ice are raging almost everywhere else.

It rains, violently but rather briefly, at Saint-Tropez and at Nice, an average of twenty to twenty-two days between December and March, in other words, for a period of three months, and temperatures for the same period range between 50° and 55° F—10 to 12 centigrades—(it's warmer in December than in February, and in March it rains appreciably more at Nice than in December). The thermometer can climb above 86° F (30° C) during the daylight hours in winter, but it drops precipitously as soon as the sun goes down. In all seasons, the frequency and force of the winds decrease progres-sively as you go east.

*
* *

Nowhere, however, do men, the earth, the sky, the climate, the vegetation, the landscape seem more cut out for pleasure and the comforts of life in the serene profusion of an endless azure and the vibrant intensity of the trium-phant sun, so that even death, when it comes, is made more clement.

Here is perhaps the rarest moment of the whole Golden Legend of the Pro-vençal coast. Precisely because it bursts forth in the very heart of winter when, under a subdued azure sky, the Mediterranean no longer has large eddies as it did during the autumn, when the January light streams down in the almost total absence of winds, and when the pale waters of the sea, in the moderately cool air, send to the coast only a weak surf, which peacefully nibbles at the shore.

Because in the near-by hills, prior to appearing in the markets, anemones, narcissuses and jonquils have begun since Christmastime to cover the fragrant, solitary and rocky "restanques," that rational cultivation of the slopes through the construction of steps, made with low, dry-stone walls, for the crops. Because, in the image of the silent season, the French Riviera seems at that time to go to sleep, to hold itself in reserve, unconcerned, sluggish, as if still sensitive to the cold; that's forgetting why for more than two hundred years the Riviera has seemed so precious, even miraculous, to the point of being preferred during that season to any other time of year.

The calm was only an illusion. All of a sudden the great brass of the Provençal symphony explode: fanfares of tall, golden bouquets sprung up from a whole year's long wait, gorged with sun, nourished by the water of the autumn rains.

At first their appearence as brilliant winter soloists touches, honors only a few scattered gardens, roads or walks, flanking "bastides" (country-houses) and villas, among the persistent — in other words, eternal — foliage of the palm-trees, eucalyptuses, pines, pepper-plants and cypresses. Suddenly, starting from the small hill of the village of Bormes, set back from the coast, whose universal fame they have henceforth established, they begin to grow without bounds in number and volume, invading neighboring heights, slopes, summits, valleys, to the point of forming a legendary forest; in the Esterel, at a stone's throw from the sea, they cover, carpet entire mountain-sides, digging in in the slightest spaces where the rock allows them to take root.

One must see at least once the flowering of the great winter mimosas on the coast of Provence. There is probably nothing like it, unless it's the fabulous pomp of the Majorca almond-trees at the same time of year. The magnificent reign, marking the thunderous awakening of Mediterranean nature, extends for a period of three to four weeks, sometimes five; and then, it's glorious.

Inexhaustible fountains of gold tumble down over the quays, the squares, the fields, the cloisters the streets, the roofs, the sea. Cities and country-side, from the suburbs of Marseilles to the tip of Cape Martin, beam in unison with the incredible miracle of their royal verdure, high stalks in full bloom and luxuriant, set in even more violent contrast by the dark green foliage which holds up their golden snow. This dazzling flow is the enchantment, the fairyland of January. (Unfortunately, the "end" of the mimosas, after Austerlitz, it's the Berezina: one by one the sumptuous golden beads, consumed by their own ardor, wither and waste so as to afford only the

42 Ramatuelle.

43-44 Port-Grimaud.

45 Sainte-Maxime.

46 Cogolin.

47 Saint-Aygulf.

48 Repairing
the fishing-nets.

49 Saint-Raphaël.

50 Draguignan.

→

51 Thoronet Abbey.

52-53 Fréjus. The arena.
The cloister.

54 *Estérel. Cap Roux Point.*

55 *Miramar.*

56 *Off Théoule.*

57 *La Napoule.*

58 *Port-la-Galère.*

59 *Cannes. La Croisette.*

distressing sight of charred, sooty clumps from which, heart-broken, one looks away.)

But immediately in the footsteps of the mimosas, blossoms appear with lightning speed on the almond-trees, second *miracle* of the Mediterranean winter. It sometimes happens, however, that the order is reversed, as a result of exceptionally stable winter temperatures, or else because a too rainy autumn has postponed the flowering of the mimosas; sometimes the two are simultaneous, and then it's the occasion for an extraordinary scramble, a joyous rivalry between the hill-sides, the orchards of the country-side and the gardens of the public walks, the villas and the hotels.

The Mediterranean landscape changes imperceptibly with the fluctuation of the seasons, but it is in the spring—which doesn't always necessarily correspond to the edicts of the calendar—that it passes most radically from the threshold of one season to the brilliance and frenzy of the next.

This means that on the Mediterranean you should expect to be in March as you would be elsewhere in May. The evened plane-trees with their stumps ominously bare since December, sole and rather rare vestige of the barren season in that region, have recovered their royal and shady foliage. At the same time, the strange, purple clusters of the Judas trees, with their pathetic first leaves all shiny, already glazed, spring up beneath the soft, immutable sky; in less than a week cherry-trees, peach-trees and apricot-trees in the Hyères or Fréjus Plains have passed from the flower stage to overburdening vegetation full of promise; tulips and peonies follow suit, all the orchards are in full bloom, the grass is thick and quivering, the swallows return, which formerly would dig themselves in until autumn in the refuge of the "genoises" (ornamental borders in tile), their shrill calls like a metallic saw percing the air above hills covered with broom—gold and emerald—in the proclamed omnipotence of the new saps.

To the magnificence of the mimosas and almond-trees of January, answers the prodigious leap forward, the amazing commotion, the hurly-burly of May, the royal month, sovereign month of flowers and fruit, of all flowers and all fruit, in the fragance of spring, then at its peak, the moving and dazzling architecture of the clouds wandering slowly at the edge of the shore—culminating in the profusion, the fireworks, the glorious "festival," the *extravagance* of roses, of all sorts of roses distributed in abundance; these barely anticipate the enchanted spring of the olive-trees, which form dust clouds, their snow scattered at their feet: this is their way of flowering, according to a tradition of modesty thousands of years old... And here's the summer.

It's here, and very much here; it fulminates, blazes, streams, that season of fire from which, only a short time ago, those very people turned away who claimed with the most exclusive and fervent ardor the "discovery" of the Sun Coast. In fact, the Riviera summer is above all the survival of the season that just preceded it; and how could it be otherwise? In Mediterranean Provence, the spring, which has marked the triumphal blossoming of the southern-French flora, had not represented, as in other northern countries, the announcement, the prologue of the season which would follow: here the summer is simply the glorious prolongation of the spring. May on the French Riviera is like July elsewhere.

Contrary to what might be suggested by the pomp and the very luxuriance of the Mediterranean vegetation at this time of year, it is indeed between June and September that the natural flora of the Provençal coast proceeds with its legitimate annual halt, a rest earned a thousand times over.

It no longer grows, nor branches out, nor multiplies nor gets stronger; it slips slowly but surely into a sleep as tranquil as it is delightful. Under the sudden lava flow of sun and heat, everything which lives fixed to the ground by roots, theoretically deprived of water during those summer months, observes a time of respite, gives itself over to a luminous, static glory. The high temperatures are not the sign, and even less the cause, of an exuberance carried to its ultimate extreme, but, on the contrary, the mark of a natural pause and stabilization.

At what other time do all the wild perfumes of the Provençal coast attain to a comparable glory—triumph—and nobility? Since the sun is more intense than at any other time of year, the aromatic plants saturate the atmosphere with emanations all the more powerful for being continuously subjected to the crushing force of the summer light. For miles out to sea, the fragrance of the summer hills comes to strike with blissful amazement the navigators cruising off the Hyères or Lérins Islands, Cape Ferrat or the coast of the Maures.

It would be surprising if the summer tourist did not receive immediately the shock of two of the most subtle perfumes in the pungent olfactory symphony of the Provençal summer along the sea coast: rose-laurels and mimosas. The former bloom starting in early June, lasting sometimes even beyond the end of summer and nowhere, certainly, with more brilliance than on the shores of the Maures Massif and on Porquerolles Island; the latter, in spite of their name, should not be taken for a case of resurrecting the distant winter.

Joseph Kessel has painted—superbly—the dazzling picture of that apotheosis of giant rose-laurels in full bloom in the most famous of the three Hyères

BYSTANDER

60-61-62 Cannes. *The beach - Swimming-pool at the Majestic - Le Suquet seen from the port.*

Islands at the peak of summer: in the deafening tumult of the cicadas, "which seems to be, even that, a sizzling of the sun... fabulous candelabras lined up and softly aglow for an endless triumphal procession." Neglecting their name, they blaze in bright red, in salmon pink—and even in white! They don't only blaze: a powerful and penetrating vanilla fragrance is emitted by the clumps of fairy-like trees at that time of day when, worn out from heat and light, they are getting ready to rock in the languid summer twilight.

As for the mimosas, that's another matter: there exist two distinctly different kinds on the coast of Provence, which are distinguished by their appearance as well as by the perfume which emanates from their foliage; they could not possibly be confused. The first flower only in winter and never appear again throughout the year. The others, on the contrary, bloom on four different occasions, punctually every three months, whence their name, mimosas of the "four seasons." Their foliage is longer and more rectangular, their clusters not so finely chiseled, so fleecy; however, their fragrance is stronger and more full-bodied, with a more sustained aroma; overheated by the July sun, they symbolize the very fragrance of the summer and, even more, that of the summer vacation in the Mediterranean sun.

Gradually after July the sparkling summer with its dreadfully high temperatures will negotiate its turn and begin to glide towards autumn, which could be called the October spring. But not, however, without having paid its tribute to the two scourges which rage, in different degrees and depending on the year, along the Provençal coast: fires (principally in the forest of the Esterel and the Maures) and the erratic wind which, coming up fiercely, often "busts" the season in two.

The former are always more or less related to the latter: though the wind does not start them, it fans them and keeps them going, sometimes all the way to total disaster. The absence of rain for the last several months, the dryness of the ground's surface and the particular vulnerability of Mediterranean flora favor the birth and spread of these fiery tempests, fatal to a country, its forests, its vegetation, even its people (you will remember the tragedy of 1970, above Cannes, which cost the lives of the wife and four children of Martin Gray). Only the sea is capable of stopping the scourge, that is, unless the wind changes course and spreads it across a new disaster area.

Furthermore, the wind doesn't only stir up insanely destructive fires and amplify disasters; it can also put an end, almost without appeal, to the good weather. The storms of mid-August are to be feared by vacationers—and also by natives—as much as the wind which triumphs over them and which should bring back the sun. Chasing the rains away, it does, indeed, bring back the sun, but by its very violence, which can rage for more than a week, it has cooled off the air and water, plucked a few trees, dried out gardens; swept by strong gusts of wind, the least protected beaches become empty. And then, September is ushered in, mild but cooler, still favorable for sun-bathing, less systematically so for sea-bathing. And the end of vacation has come.

Between 1970 and 1975, there was a strange summer when the storks suddenly appeared at the height of a torrid heat-wave, announcing an early winter; they only rested a brief moment at the mouth of the Var, near Nice, after a flight which brought them back towards more temperate regions. Their passage, in the middle of the dog days, foreshadowed weeks of particularly severe winter. And already this prospect gave everyone the shivers.

The rose-laurels have ended their flowering, which has lasted from June to the end of August; the purple or scarlet bougainvilleas have continued with theirs, which will last through the autumn and often through the winter; the exuberant, climbing clumps of plumbagos with blue flowers, more rarely white, escort them along-side the villas; the fringes of marvels-of-Peru, red, yellow, white and violet, which open only at nightfall, will survive October, sometimes even November, mixing their heady emanations with those of the flowering branches of the orange-trees.

In the bluish hills of autumn, with its still long and luminous days, pounded by the great sea swells and their vast coats of foam, it's the moment when the plants of the Mediterranean coast will awaken, finally, from their deep summer sleep, favored by the appearance of the first torrential rains. November has arrived.

The reputation of autumn on the Mediterranean suffers, it's true, from the memories attached to the fleeing pleasures of summer, still so near and which have only been really enjoyed for the last forty years; however, the mediocrity of the season from October to December is not unalterable, even if the process itself is indisputably so: from Marseilles to Menton, it's the sea-wind which brings the rain and it's the other wind, blowing fiercely from the mountains, which chases it away, but which in turn only dies down with the help of a shower of "a few drops." In autumn, as also now and then in spring, it sometimes happens that the "few drops" are transformed into a deluge.

Beautiful gilded and reddish autumns do exist in Mediterranean southern France, as well as in the Ile-de-France (Paris region), on the Loire or the

63-64-65 *Lérins Islands.*
The monastery on Saint-Honorat.
The fortress on Sainte-Marguerite.
The fortress on Saint-Honorat.

66 Grasse. Place aux Aires.

67-68 Escragnolles, village where the Emperor stopped.- Route Napoléon.

69 Grand Canyon of the Verdon. Vaumale Circus. - 70 Castellane.
71. Moustiers-Sainte-Marie. - 72 Verdon. Samson Corridor.

73 Antibes. Fortifications
by Vauban.

74-75 Saint-Paul-
de-Vence. Fountain.
Maeght Foundation,
sculptures by Giacometti.

76 Loup Gorges.
Courmes Cascade.

77 Tourette-sur-Loup.
Picking violets.

78-79
Cagnes-sur-Mer.
Renoir Museum.
Patio of the
castle-museum.

80 Vallauris.
Pottery.

banks of the Garonne or the Rhone; but it is often a good bet that a glorious autumn will be followed by a winter either less brilliant or else more severe. From a strong and ancient wisdom derived from sober lessons learned, Provençal fishermen and horticulturists have drawn this maxim: *Everything must be paid for.*

*
* *

From the wonder of the sun, a collective adventure, and from touring, a social fact, was born one day the French Riviera, geographic phenomenon, seabord section of that great Provence of the olive-trees and the Mistral (north wind), and at the same time a reality, an institution which is always, in spite of everything, a little artificial—like those operetta principalities of which Monaco remains, today, the smiling vestige, the pure and anachronistic jewel.

The name of Tobias George Smolett would have deserved to remain famous, for it is he, translator of Voltaire and author of *Travels through France and Italy, with a particular description of the city, the territory and the climate of Nice,* who aroused his English compatriots over two centuries ago, to come and bathe in the waters of the Mediterranean.

And yet, he hadn't been especially kind to Nice servant-girls, whom he found "lazy, neglectful and repulsively dirty," nor to Nice shopkeepers, whom he judged to be "greedy and dishonest," nor to Nice workers and artisans, "who think only of warming themselves in the sun," nor to Nice streets, "full of excrements," nor to Nice houses, with their windows "covered with paper instead of glass panes," nor to Nice flies, flees and bed-bugs, "swooping down in clouds, day and night, even into my cup of tea!"

But Smolett, the inventor of sea-bathing on the beaches of the County of Nice, had seen something else: the sun "as hot as in England in May, although it's the middle of winter and in the morning there's frost on the ground." And the lemon-trees, the orange-trees, the woods of olive-trees, the fields of carnations. Not to mention the local gastronomy: anchovies deep-fried in oil, watermelons, wines from Saint-Laurent-du-Var. And the traveler couldn't help but exclaim: *It rains so seldom!*

Following Smolett, other Englishmen landed on the shores of Nice in such crowds that the visitor accomodations of the small city promptly revealed their insufficiency. It became necessary to begin construction of a new hotel, which was named, quite naturally, Hôtel d'Angleterre (Hotel of England).

That's not all. It was characteristic that the compatriots of Tobias George Smolett in no way sought to mix with the local population, but on the contrary, showed a distinct tendency to concentrate in perfectly impermeable colonies: gathering together at tea-time, collecting to comment on the news from the London papers or to stroll along the sea.

Though the English weren't alone, nevertheless, they were all that you saw. Seventy years later Dumas observed that for the inhabitants of Nice any traveler can only be English, although it is hard to say whether those Englishmen "aren't French or German." Since they had become accustomed to meet in the sun while chatting and walking along the sea, a long terrace was built along the edge of the shore; it was named, quite naturally, Promenade des Anglais (Walkway of the English). It's fair to say that they've never really stopped honoring it since.

The history of the French Riviera is the history of ten cities, of a hundred towns, of a thousand hamlets and villages, added to 125 miles (200 km) of sea coast, whose fortune was most often made by chance, and which have, one and all, a solid common denominator: the sun, which—in a temperate region—generally implies a relatively tolerable climate. An Englishman had launched Nice, at that time a Sardinian territory which wasn't permanently annexed by France until a century later; another Englishman launched Cannes.

His name was Brougham; he was a peer, and Lord-Chancelor of Great Britain; he was on his way to spend the winter at Nice, but he was prevented from entering by the military police of the King of Sardinia, who were stationed in a sanitary cordon on the frontier of the Var. In 1834, southern France was ravaged by an epidemy of cholera—the cholera of *Le Hussard sur le toit (The Soldier on the Roof)* by Giono—, and the orders of the Turin government were to drive away all travelers without exception in order to protect the Sardinian States from the spread of the plague.

Like an ordinary private citizen, Lord Brougham was kept away by the Nice constabulary. He was furious, as much at having to submit to a foreign will as at having to forego his pleasures and his plans. He was nevertheless

81-82 *Vallauris. "The man with the sheep," bronze by Picasso. Castle chapel, painting by Picasso, "War and Peace."*

83 *Biot. Fernand Léger Museum, detail from the mosaic before the façade.*

84 *Vence. Rosary Chapel decorated by Matisse.*

forced to turn around. At dusk he came within sight of Cannes, and entranced, captivated, he suddenly ordered his carriage to stop: before him was the sea, the sand, the Lérins Islands, the violet chain of the Esterel in the setting sun. The mortifying disappointment of Nice, the affront suffered on the banks of the Var, the cholera were all forgotten. He slept at the Poste-aux–Chevaux (Poney Express) Inn, not without having sat down to eat the first "bouillabaisse" (Provençal fish-soup) of his existence, prepared before his eyes and composed of sixteen varieties of fish!

Despite the vigilance of the police, the cholera didn't spare the Sardinian territories. But Brougham, who was counting on only spending one night at Cannes, would stay there the rest of his life. Following a strictly similar process, the same phenomenon of animation and colonization by sojourning tourists which the Baie des Anges (Bay of Angels) had witnessed seventy years before was renewed in the shade of Le Suquet.

This time, however, the winter migration set in motion by the example of the Chancelor of England saw an implantation on the whole more distinctly aristocratic, with its inevitable and immediate corollary: among the palm-trees, the pine forests and the mimosas, a phenomenal flowering of villas, residences, castles with *Made in England* lawns, in varied styles—quite varied—, of which the property of the noble lord was the first of all. It is not surprising that the statue erected by public contributions to the memory of Henry Peter Brougham bears, engraved in gold, a violent, lyric hommage to the modern founder of Cannes, who *stands, his finger pointing to the earth... entwining round a palm-tree the rose of England;* these verses are by one of his most enthousiastic followers, Stephen Liégeard.

The originators of Riviera vacationing, the English of Nice had their Pro-menade (dating from 1820); at Cannes there was only a local soap-factory, whose director, wishing to get rid of cumbersome material, had it taken to the sea-shore, where it gradually piled up until it finally formed a sort of coastal road on which the winter vacationers came to watch the fishermen return into port; it was named La Croisette.

When the construction of the railroad was begun around 1860, the Paris-Lyons-Marseilles Train Company proposed to have transported to La Croisette the earth and rock debris resulting from work on the line, on the condition that they be compensated at the rate of .06 centimes per cubic meter. Cannes' city council accepted this arrangement, and Lord Brougham, who had just begun his eighty-first year, saw the road become a boulevard, which it still is (the *rue d'Antibes;* at that time it was the *route d'Italie*).

Meanwhile, another revolution was brewing; it had even broken out, and, strangely enough, its instigator was a crowned sovereign. It took place well to the east of Cannes, about thirty miles (50 km) from La Croisette, more precisely, between Nice and Menton.

The Grimaldi dynasty is one of the oldest in Europe, probably the only one to have reigned without interruption from the thirteenth century right up to the present day. Although their government seems to be built on a rock—a rock washed by the sea—, and although they received their title of Princes of Monaco from a King of Spain, as far back as their origins trace the Grimaldi have known brilliance, glory and ruin, revolutions, abductions and blood: John II killed by his brother Lucien, Lucien assassinated by his nephew Doria, Honoré I thrown into the sea by his subjects and Honoré IV drowned in the Seine, the complementary military occupations of Spain and France, the revolt of the fiefs of Roquebrune and Menton, which were carved off from the Principality...

In 1848 the house of Grimaldi was represented by Prince Floristan I, whose name and title made him worthy to furnish Sacha Guitry with the subject of an operetta. He hadn't married a princess, but a "respectable girl" of the middle class, a princess in spite of herself, just as he was a prince in spite of himself, after having been a singer at the Ambigu-Comique Theater, just as his wife had been, so they say, a dancer. And neither one was interested in anything besides their music and water-color painting. This was not sufficient to assure their state a balanced budget, the endemic torture of the Princes of Monaco for generations past.

After the secession of Roquebrune and Menton, which deprived the Treasury of its income from the citrus-fruit trade and reduced the dimensions of the Principality to the scant 250 acres (100 hectares) it had had originally, Prince Floristan made his decision and laid down a bothersome crown in favor of his son, the future Charles III. It is Charles who was the revolutionary.

He didn't beat around the bush. If he had imposed new taxes, without fail his reign would have quickly become unpopular, which he didn't want, even though the time was long past when the people of Monaco threw their sovereigns from atop their rock into the Mediterranean. He decided that Monaco, sovereign capital of a miniature state, would become a *gaming house,* and on December 14, 1856, between the walls of a low, smoke-filled room with the shady look of a gambling-den, rang out for the first time the famous cry: "Place your bets! The betting is closed!"

85 *Perched village of*
Le Castellet-les-Sausses.

86 *Puget-Théniers.*

87 *Entrevaux.*

88 *Enriez.*

97-98-99 Nice.   Houses along the port - Promenade des Anglais - Russian Orthodox Cathedral.

100 La Turbie.
Trophy of Augustus.

101 Saint-Antoine-
de-Siga.

102 Horse-back riding
near Valdeblore.

The "revolution" of Charles III was completed, and with it was sealed—in installments and with a boost from a French financier, a native of the Landes named François Blanc—the incredible fortune of the Most Serene Princes of Monaco, of their Rock and of the people of Monaco themselves.

Since 1863, the Paris train arrived regularly in the Cannes Station, and the travelers could continue their journey all the way to Cagnes-sur-Mer, the end of the prestigious line joining the capital with the Mediterranean. As soon as he had taken into his hands the destiny of Monaco's gambling, Mr. Blanc entered into talks with the Paris-Lyons-Marseilles Train Company and was fortunate enough to succeed in these negotiations, which for the first time brought the railroad into the territory of the Principality, increasing to a very considerable extent the influx of tourists and devotees of games of chance—at a time when baccara, roulette and blackjack tables were universally outlawed throughout the territory of France (by an order of Louis Philippe renewed by Napoleon III).

Since the old gambling hall of 1856, which was dirty and foul-smelling, had been transferred to the other side of the valley of La Condamine, to the terrace of the Spélugues Plateau at the foot of Mount Agel, the successor of Floristan I was able to see, erected little by little across from his princely rock, a new capital, rising from the stone and the sea with its tens of hotels, its hundreds of residences and villas, its streets, its boulevards, its squares, its gardens and its monumental *casino*. Astonishing, unexpected, wonderous, richer, more populated, even more grandiose than the former capital, fantastic, fabulous nurturer, it was the symbol of the resurrection and modern prosperity of Monaco and the Grimaldi princes. They finally had to give it a name, and since Floristan's son was named Charles, they called it Monte-Carlo.

Naturally, Mr. François Blanc and the princes were bound by a contract. It established the Sea-bathing and Foreigners' Club Company, and it is still in force. This contract, or rather its consequence, the gambling revenue from Monte-Carlo, would allow Prince Charles III to make his faithful subjects very happy by granting them a privilege, a remarkable exemption, almost unparalleled: starting in 1869, the fortunate people of Monaco would no longer pay taxes.

A century later, this princely liberality is also still in force. In addition, although a 1918 agreement, while preserving the autonomy of Monaco, recognizes France as heir to the Grimaldis in case the dynasty should become extinct, citizens of the Principality are exempt from military service.

Today there are scarcely more than two thousand people who can claim the benefit of this double dispensation. However, following the crisis with France in 1962, which seemed for a time to threaten the independence of Monaco, a fiscal accord provided that all French citizens who had lived in the Principality for five years or less would be subject to the same taxation as their fellow countrymen.

Exempt from military service and freed from direct taxation, the people of Monaco, obedient subjects of His Most Serene Highness the Sovereign Prince, must submit, however, to a single, imperative obligation, with which, for once, the French government has nothing to do, but which the prudent Charles III clearly stipulated in his agreement with François Blanc: never to go sit down around the fabulous green-covered gaming tables of their famous casino which, still today, they are categorically forbidden to enter, admission being strictly reserved for the foreign clientele.

What Blanc had done for Monaco, Brougham for Cannes and Smolett for Nice, a fourth man would do sixty years later between Nice and Cannes.

Unlike—and yet so near—the coast of the Languedoc, with its vast strands of fine sand brought and deposited through the ages, the coast of Provence, rocky, almost everywhere jagged, with its wooded hills immediately overhanging the shore, has practically none of those long, gilded beaches, but rather coves with scant sand and the many projections of the coastal contour between Marseilles and Menton. The two beaches of Cavalaire and Pampelonne in the Var are the exception; from the Esterel on, the Riviera is so lacking in beaches that those with natural sand could be counted on the fingers of one hand.

Even the beach at Cannes, sumptuous, dazzling behind the Bay of La Napoule, is the result of persistent and costly efforts mounted from 1885 to the present. In other words, the beach is artificial, created by constructing jetties designed to retain the sand and then by dumping vast quantities of hard sand brought from out at sea or from the mouth of the Siagne; the process continued well beyond the end of the war in 1945. (Moreover, the process has been used in numerous other places along the coast, but with less success, however: it will take years before the supplementary quarry-sand, infinitely less burdensome to obtain, is replaced, through the effect of the sea-currents and the action of weak tides, by sea-sand.)

Now, though sand was extremely rare on the French Riviera, particularly between Menton and Saint-Raphaël, nevertheless it did exist in one place,

103
Roquebrune-Cap-Martin.

which was neither Cannes nor Nice, but which was situated precisely between these two cities, these meccas of the thriving Mediterranean tourist-trade. It was around 1924 that this realization was made by an American billionaire, son of the railroad king of the western United States, by the name of Gould.

The place where Mr. Gould made his interesting discovery was situated precisely at the flank of the Cape of Antibes along a rather wide coastal strip where, more than a century before, March 1, 1815, Napoleon Bonaparte had trod on the sand on his return from Elba, while uttering his famous and fateful proclamation: "The eagle will fly with the national colors from steeple to steeple all the way to the towers of Notre Dame!" A large pine forest covered the shores behind Gulf Juan, and the free and happy profusion of these trees had given its name to a sea-side locality (population 1,727): Juan-les-Pins.

Frank Jay Gould wasn't the only person, nor the first, to focus his attention on the privileged nature of the beach at Juan-les-Pins, nor to calculate the advantage to which such a remarkable site could be turned. At Nice, pebbles were triumphant; elsewhere gravel; in still other places, debris of porphyry or rock. At Juan reigned alone, without a rival from Antibes to Menton, the hot, golden sand and the pines.

For four years, from 1914 to 1918, trains with the Allied wounded had streamed towards the Mediterranean coast and, requisitioned, the modest casino of Juan-les-Pins had been turned into a military hospital. After the war, a hotel-keeper from Nice, Edouard Baudoin, bought back this casino for a song, acquired some land along the sea-shore and opened a restaurant. While watching a (silent) American film, Baudoin had been struck by the beach of Miami covered with sun-bathers, and that had given him an idea.

This idea coincided with the thinking which Mr. Gould had been doing on the same spot, and the two men, destined to reach an understanding, exploited it jointly, the Frenchman contributing his experience and knowledge of the region, the American his relations and capital. Just as Tobias George Smolett had promoted sea-bathing in the Mediterranean, Gould and Baudoin launched, with a noble audacity, the fashion of sun-bathing on the Mediterranean shores. And since the sun really heats up the sand only at the time of year when it stands at the zenith of its course, the summer season on the French Riviera was launched—invented.

This was the fourth metamorphosis, and probably not the last, which helped to finally and truly make, of a privileged portion of the Provençal sea-shore, the French Riviera.

From then on, the sun of southern France would, so to speak, shine all year round. And in fact, very soon—the ten years separating 1925 from 1935 constitute a relatively short space of time with respect to a history which was already sixteen times longer—it would start shining for everyone.

Step by step, the extraordinary vogue of the Sun Coast hadn't stopped growing, expanding in proportion to the development of the means of transportation which, for their part, made a prodigious leap forward, thus making more accessible a more ardently coveted paradise. This vogue even overflowed the traditional boundaries of the enchanted kingdom: Toulon and Hyères were closer to Paris by train; Saint-Tropez and Sainte-Maxime in the Maures, where Colette settled down, were no longer considered such excentric vacation spots compared to the winter resorts and sea resorts of the Esterel and the Alpes-Maritimes.

August 2, 1931 marked the historic date on which the high authorities of the Riviera hotel industry, assembled in war council, decreed that from then on their establishments *would no longer close during the summer*.

However, the great revolution of the French Riviera would proceed directly from another revolution, this one political, the coming to power of the French leftist parties, that is, the advent of the Popular Front and the establishment, starting in the summer of 1936, of paid vacations extended to all categories of workers. With one stroke, a new social class gained access to the first fruits of the civilization of leisure.

From then on, the summer *rush* could no longer be stopped; it should legitimately be called "the second-wave vogue." After seventy-three years, the French Riviera had finally won the battle of summer. However, for a long time this victory would be only theoretical and temporary.

The progressive shift in seasonal frequentation of the Happy Coast took place at the same time that the new character of this frequentation was becoming apparent. At first it had been confined essentially to winter, then it was extended partially to summer, being reserved in both cases to a clientele of tourists and sojourners which was rather markedly patrician and often foreign, able to take advantage of the privileges and titles conferred on it by birth, fortune and notoriety.

At this time, from 1936 to 1939, the clivage between the two seasons became even sharper, and this time it had an indisputable social significance. The winter coast remained in favor with the more well-to-do, leisured "smart society," that *high society* which one day, after a war with a nuclear epilogue, would give birth to the *jet set*, tha society eagerly seeking *la dolce vita* in all latitudes. The other coast, that of summer, moved towards a clientele which was predominently lower middle-class and working-class with limited budgets. "Minks against two-piece bathing-suits."

This demographic division of the Vacation and Joy-of-Living Coast, at least as much a consequence of the evolution in manners as of the politico-financial crisis between the wars, would seal, sooner or later and more or less brutally, the defeat of the great Mediterranean palaces before the whirl-wind assault of the close-ranked infantry of modest hotels and furnished apartments, pending the offensive of trailer-homes and intensive camping.

This clivage would even survive the end of World War II, until a new era dawned which would overturn all ancient data on the seasonal displacement of people, sweeping away barriers and mercilessly striking down customs—by a convergence of the unheard of and revolutionary policy of staggered vacations, the advent of co-ownership, the proliferation of second homes and of large apartment and tourist complexes, private automobiles and pleasure boats no less privately owned, henceforth putting the sanctuaries of the sun within year-round reach of all pocketbooks.

*
* *

In the night between August 14 and 15, 1944, the war penetrated unexpectedly into Provence, between Toulon and Cannes, igniting its battles on the flank of the French Riviera, from Cape Nègre, near Le Lavandou, to the tip of Point Esquillon, near Le Trayas, while inland it was falling from the sky in the vicinity of Le Muy, near Draguignan. It was Operation Dragon.

Mid-summer 1944: seventy days before, the Allies had got a foothold on the coasts of Normandy. Thus the invasion across the Mediterranean, strictly complementary to that of June 6 across the English Channel, met a precise goal: to trap the greatest possible number of German troops in France in an irresistable vise, in order to anihilate them, prior to the onslaught of Eisenhower's armies towards their final objective, the heart

116 Menton.

97

of Germany. Two months and a week after June 6, one of the jaws of the vise existed in Normandy; the debarcation of August 15 in Provence represented the other one.

While the 1,200 ships of the Allied armada in the Mediterranean shut off their engines, facing the front of attack, to wait for daylight, isolated units of commandos and paratroopers landed on the coast of Provence with an identical purpose: to lock up the attack zone before H-Hour, in order to deny the German divisions of southern France all access routes leading to the future beach-head.

Six hundred artillery pieces of all calibers awaited the assailants, bristling on the capes, sprinkled across the rock and sand, hanging over the beaches, capping the crests, from Marseilles to Nice.

In the Provençal night, where a belated crescent-moon is hanging, the night breath of the near-by land, the wild perfumes of the Mediterranean summer, the odors of eucalyptus and pine, of plants heated until dusk by the August sun, reach the 300,000 American, French, Canadian and English soldiers filling the immense battle fleet, the most fantastic steel hull ever borne by the Mediterranean.

On land, since early evening, a "message" as sibylline as it is "personal" has preceded the new-comers, announcing the imminence of the assault to the clandestine combattants of the Resistance in Provence: *Nancy has a crick in her neck...*

Finally the night brightened, the day of August 15 dawned, and the sun rose rapidly on the 175th anniversary of the birth of Napoleon I. At 8:00 am, H-Hour of D-Day Provence, a fog you could cut with a knife covered the beaches and the coastal hills torn up by hours of bombardment (an average of a ton of bombs every sixty-five feet—20 m— had been dropped on the thirty miles—50 km—of the attack front).

Under the pines blasted by artillery fire and in swirls of thick, dull smoke, the 20,000 men of the assaulting wave, veterans of the battles of Africa and Italy, jumped from their boats before the beaches of Cavalaire, Pampelonne, La Nartelle, Val-d'Esquières, Le Dramont and Anthéor.

The battle under the pines, amidst the vines of the Maures Massif and in the red rocks of the Esterel, lasted all morning and part of the afternoon. At nightfall the Provence beach-head extended about ten miles (15 km) inland from the coast and over almost all of the Hyères Islands, and the Allied flags were flying at Saint-Tropez, Sainte-Maxime and Saint-Raphaël. Around Draguignan the vise of airborne troops was tightening its hold.

Another night passed, and then another day. And the dusk descended, which, for tens of thousands of soldiers at sea, would be unlike any other. These were the soldiers of the French divisions, the bulk of the invading army, seven-tenths of it, to be precise, mobilized in Algeria, Tunisia and Morocco, of which four out of seven divisions came directly from the Italian front after the battles of Cassino, Rome and Sienna. They constituted the First Army of General De Lattre de Tassigny who, if Giraud and De Gaulle had had their way with the Allied general staff, would have commanded the landing forces in Provence, in place of the American General Patch.

Restlessly prancing out at sea and impatient to return home after four years of absence, they had heard on the open sea the shock of bombs and shells crashing down on the coast, between Cavalaire and Anthéor; they had seen units of the French Navy taking part in the battle of D-Day Provence, alongside the American and British fleets, and they also knew that, during the night of warefare preceding the general assault, the first of all the Allied soldiers to set foot in France, in the rocks of Cape Nègre and at Point Esquillon, had been French. It so happened that the first killed were, too. Now their long armed watch was coming to a close.

This return to their country, under the victorious flags hoisted on the masts of the Allied fleet, was a moment which these men wouldn't forget. And it took place like this: everyone was standing around De Lattre and his principal lieutenants on the decks, near the guard-rails; the sun was getting ready to go down; on the Mediterranean glided the pearly light of a summer evening as they exist only on the coast of Provence. In the distance, land appeared on the horizon: it was France.

Those were the men who, on August 28, surrounded Toulon and Marseilles, liberated the same day. Cannes had been liberated two days before; Nice would be two days later.

All the same, it was very strange and surprising, that war under the pines and, precisely, in a setting where it is hard to imagine: the palm-trees waving in the blue sky of August, the immense battle front attacked head-on by the sun, directly above the shore, a long, wet band of seaweed mixed with the thick, gray ash of battle, the heavy perfume of the Maures and the Esterel... And when the troops had got a foothold on the shore, between the sporadic shell-fire and the crackle of machine-guns, the prodigious, immense song, the endless chirping of the cicadas.

Three weeks and five days after August 15, two months and a week after June 66, Allied soldiers who had landed in Provence joined forces, on National Highway 71 between Dijon and Troyes, with those that had landed in Normandy.

*
* *

The Coast, the South, southern France, that profuse Mediterranean which the rest of Europe envies those who live there, the invitation to travel and all the charms of a sunny paradise: for a long time, the French Riviera represented the country where the Blue Train went.

That could be its modern definition, after Tobias Smolett discovered it and Stepen Liégeard christened it.

That is also what it has remained. On it, since then, has, quite naturally, converged a network of major highways in pursuit of the sun, starting with the very famous, very much coveted National 7, which plunged down from Paris and which, section after segment, has been greatly reinforced by the opening of the Southern Expressway, triumphal route, which now puts the capital seven hours away from the shores of the Mediterranean.

This combined stimulus of railroad and highway has sufficed to make of the French Riviera and its magic shores, starting in the fifties, the most populated region in France from June to September, beside that legendary *Mare nostrum*, the most beautiful sea in the world become the great vacation bath-tub.

Whatever the means used to get there, road vehicule or train, there is probably no more privileged moment than that in which the traveler's gaze falls for the first time, after hours on the road or a whole night's journey by railway, through the door of a railway car, an automobile or a bus, on the blue, scintillating horizon of the enchanted sea.

By train, this event takes place as you enter the La Ciotat Station (after a fleeting view of the islands of Marseilles just before the suburbs of the Phocian metropolis coming from Avignon and Arles by way of Miramas). By direct highway, the traveler must wait until Saint-Raphaël and the glorious entrance to the country of the Great Blue Vacation Sea, all vibrant with its celebrity.

Like the railway, the highways systematically avoid passing through the Maures Massif; but should this really be lamented? As if the lay-outs of highways and railroads had attended to urgent matters first by plunging with ever more impatience towards the Rivieran East, they have completely neglected a whole portion of coast between Toulon and Saint-Raphaël, particularly from Hyères to Saint-Tropez.

But in its misfortune at being insufficiently served, this coast has fortunately gained thereby: honored only by the very secondary National 559 along the sea-side, the Maures Corniche, developing its sprightly string of sea-resort towns with their gay and piquant names, from La Fossette and Saint-Clair to Aiguebelle, Pramousquier (the "Meadow Monastery") and Le Rayol, Le Dattier and Cavalaire, has thus been able to remain perhaps one of the most absolutely luxuriant regions, wooded almost to the point of suffocation, flowering and fragrant, and at the same time, one of the most miraculously preserved of the whole coast of Provence.

(Up to the end of the last war, transportation across the Maures Massif was provided by the picturesque and short-winded rail-car of the Provence Railroad, nicknamed the "pine-cone train" because during the trip the travelers had plenty of time to gather pine-cones and even, it is claimed, to engage in games of *boules* (lagging steel balls), without noticeably retarding the train's advance; today it has been replaced by a bus line which is much more expeditious.)

Saint-Tropez, which during the last quarter century has been able to justify the name of Saint-Germain-des-Prés-on-the-Sea, can be reached directly from Bormes-les-Mimosas across the sumptuous, inland Dom National Forest, paradise of chestnut-trees and of all varieties of mushrooms, by way of La Môle and its castle, family property of Saint-Exupéry; an obligatory side-trip should be made to the majestic ruins of the admirable La Verne Charterhouse, isolated in a breath-taking setting. We thus arrive at the very end of the Gulf of Saint-Tropez, in sight of the strange city of Port-Grimaud, built on piles by François Spoerry; contrary to its older sister-city Venice, automobiles are allowed to drive about, while television antennas are banned.

If you happen to be at Saint-Tropez in May, you will be surprised to hear the small city crackling with volleys of blunderbuss fire, the whole population in a holiday mood poured out into the streets or decorating the balconies and quays, in a great explosion of singing and shouting, along the route of a quaint procession mixing the truncated statue of a saint and the combined delegations of the local clergy and the city government. It's the *Bravade* (Act of defiance), one of the most popular, picturesque and famous festivals of the Provençal coast.

The saint, of course, snatched from the gentle drowsiness of his chiming sanctuary, is St. Tropez, patron of the city: a Christian centurion decapitated under Nero and cast out to sea in a bark, accompanied by a rooster and a dog which were supposed to devour him. Nothing of the kind happened. The waves miraculously pushed the boat right to the Provençal shores, to the very spot where this event is commemorated.

As a matter of fact, the remembrance of this miracle would be ill-suited to the noisy display which accompanies it, if the people of Saint-Tropez weren't celebrating at the same time the heroism of their ancestors, who, during the Thirty Years War, victoriously repulsed an attack by twenty-one Spanish galleys, represented today by twenty-one blunderbusses discharging in unison their thunder and lightning.

A whole troop can be seen, all got up and very much bent on firing in all directions, under the command of a municipal captain elected for three days by the city council: *bravadeurs* (the "defiant") and musketeers who shoot their previously blessed weapons at the patron saint, the symbol of the besieged city, prior to spreading out throughout the city, to the sound of fifes and drums, in the din of a thousand detonations. And the crackling gaiety continues for three equally explosive days—a little like the signal which has just awakened Saint-Tropez from its winter torpor, so it can face, though not repulse, another sort of invasion, that of the tourists of the coming summer.

The legendary story of St. Tropez offers a vivid similarity to another Provençal legend and is no less comparable to a third. The three Holy Women forced to flee from Judea and who, landing on the shores of the Camargue, gave their name to Saintes-Maries-de-la-Mer (Saints Mary by the Sea), recall the decapitated centurion, just as the latter brings irresistibly to mind another persecuted Christian: she, too, cast to the waves; she, too, abandoned in a bark without sail nor oars; but that was in the third century. She is St. Dévote, martyred in Corsica. Her frail skiff also ran aground in Provence, but this time in the rocks of Monaco.

But the miracle is not what you might think. Venerated, her relics were coveted in the eleventh century by a rich Florentine, who succeeded in stealing them and fleeing. However, the boat carrying the relics was unable to leave the port, thus marking the unfailing attachment of the saint to Monaco. It is this event which is celebrated every year, on January 26, with pomp and enthousiasm by the people of Monaco; it is celebrated by burning a bark on the shores.

*
* *

Here it is, the royal gate, grandiose, shaggy, without an equivalent on the whole length of the coast; such, in fact, as it is exploited to excess in hundreds and thousands of color-prints for mass-produced postcards; such, also, as all this photographic evidence attempts to reproduce it, the representation of color photography becoming equivalent, finally, to the reality which inspired it.

It is perhaps the true miracle of the Esterel not to cause disappointment, except that of proving, on the whole, a bit too consistent with what one had imagined. Here there is no fantasy, except that which everyone is free to confront and record. There will always be people who regret that things are too perfect; let's admit, then, that the French Riviera is hardly made for them. Here under the pale azure of the sky, the truly red mountain *really* plunges into the truly blue sea.

Here is the flamboyant Esterel, rocks, jagged and eroded summits, peaks, sharp crests, steep blocs of marble fantastically precipitated into the waters, sandstones and porphyries — reddish, blue, gray — of the fabulous chain.

Here is magnificence itself, plenitude, apogee, apotheosis; not, however, without a sort of haughty wildness with sinister overtones: it's not without reason that, from gorge to grotto, prowl the — quite fictitious — ghost of Robert Macaire and those — more real — of Gaspard de Besse or Mandrin, around the inn of Les Adrets, "rebuilt by Mr. Laugier, Esquire in 1653, restored in 1898," which, at some 660 feet (200 m) above sea-level, forms the whole famous hamlet of Le Logue de l'Esterel, preferred refuge of highway robbers and escapees from the Toulon prison on the look-out for stray travelers.

The Esterel begins at the Reyran Gorges, of no less sinister reputation after that terrible night of December 2, 1959, when the Malpasset Dam broke, spilling its devastating torrent on the whole western part of Fréjus, and ends at La Napoule. For crossing the lower part, it offers a liaison road, already old and which, though it goes back to the beginning of the century, nevertheless has remained triumphal for an essential reason: it doesn't leave the sea, and in places it is even emboldened to span it.

The railroad follows this route closely. In avoiding it, motorists impatient to get to Cannes or Nice run a great risk of missing the most remarkable part, a whole garland of sea-side resorts dipping into the Mediterranean: from Boulouris to Le Dramont, from Agay to Anthéor, from Le Trayas to Miramar (which means "admire the sea") and to Théoule. The name generally used to designate it hardly ever appears on ordinary maps, although it is not usurped. It is called the Golden Corniche.

At water-level, they seem like brother and sister, he having rejected all haughtiness, accepting the tutelary superiority of his more opulent younger sister, rich with the whole verdant mass of her woods of giant eucalyptuses and pines, and even with several notable elevations in terrain. Thus appear, flushed out from the episodic curves of a winding, contorted Esterel, those two islands of the Lérins Archipelago which everyone knows about since the incarceration of the Man with the Iron Mask.

Thus also, according to a legend which isn't, for all that, as legendary as they say, goes the beautiful story of St. Honorat and St. Margaret, fraternal adepts of the contemplative life in the fourth and fifth centuries. The former, Honorat, came looking for solitude amidst the waves of the Provençal coast; but this retreat became the talk of all the devotees of monastic life, and other hermits flocked there. This colony, isolated at mid-sea, became itself a religious order, and the refuge of Honorat, the future Archbishop of Arles, became a solid monastery, the Lérins Abbey which was to be one of the chief spiritual centers of barbarian Europe.

Since women were forbidden access to Honorat's island, his sister, Margaret, head of a religious community on the neighboring island, was distressed at being deprived of seeing her brother, from whom she was separated by a narrow channel, made uncrossable by the laws of religion, which counted for naught the bonds of blood. At last Honorat consented to a promise: he would visit Margaret once a year, at the flowering of the almond-trees. Now, there were no almond-trees on Margaret's island, so she hastened to plant one on the shore, and it, in turn, hastened to flower every month...

Here is Cannes the Magnificent, the most famous beach in France, whose very modern slogan — which doesn't, however, tell the whole story — *Life is beautiful in the summer at Cannes*, would certainly have plunged

Henry Peter Brougham himself into deep perplexity, but even more so the Roman centurions who, at this very place, patroled through the marsh reeds (or *cane*) of the coast, to which the city with the alabaster front, like the Canebière of Marseilles, has a very good chance of owing its name.

From the heights of Le Suquet to La Croisette Point crowned by the dazzling Palm Beach, the modern vacation capital goes from the early Middle Ages to the era of flood-lights and movie-cameras. With the latter, at the instigation of the historian Philippe Erlanger, who was also an official at the Foreign Office, Cannes has become established, for one week a year, in May, as a world capital among the most qualified to create stars and starlets, palms and laurels.

Here is Mougins, in the interior, on the way to Grasse, the city of flowers and perfume; then Vallauris, closer to the coast, the home of Provençal ceramics, of which Pablo Picasso made it, starting in 1950, one of the capitals; then Gulf-Juan and Juan-les-Pins; and Antibes, the *city opposite* (from Nice), city of roses, the "Saint-Malo of the Riviera," which, until the annexation of the County of Nice, was the first stronghold this side of the frontier; Biot and Cagnes, set inland, the one producing those legions of heavy, bulging earthenware jars which populate the terraces of all the gardens of Mediterranean southern France, the other, paradise of carnations, where Auguste Renoir came to die, suffering terribly, at the end of his life, from acute rheumatism and unable to paint except by having paint-brushes attached to his wrists; Saint-Paul-de-Vence and Vence, dazzling among the jasmines, lavanders, carnations, roses, violets, olive-trees, lemon-trees, vineyards and cypresses; Cros-de-Cagnes, on the sea... The whole sumptuous parade of meeting-places of sun and colors.

And then, over there, the Var. How could we fail to stop on the bank of this "plain of pebbles" which Tobias Smolett crossed one autumn evening in 1763, before the sandy bed where the torrential river runs into the Mediterranean, just as was forced to stop there, seventy years later, the carriage of Lord Brougham, who went elsewhere and didn't regret it? To the left, the rise of the high, tumultuous valley with steep slopes of olive-tree woods, fields of vines and flowers, the coral-like eagle's nests of a few "perched" villages, and then beyond, the snowy Alps. Straight ahead, the far end of the great gulf hollowed out from the Cape of Antibes to the promontory of Mount Boron, so marvelously called the Baie des Anges (Bay of Angels).

At last, Nice, goddess of Victory (origin disputed) and daughter by direct descent of Marseilles, Phocian both of them; home of the *pissaladière* (italianized under the more wide-spread name of *pizza*) and of the famous *soupe au pistou* (vegetable soup with herbs), of candied fruit and of noodles, of olive oil and of the *ratatouille* (eggplant casserole), and of course of the Nice (combinaison) salad; without mentioning the various applications of pyrotechnics, as well as two other indisputable industries: street-organs and player-pianos.

Here is Nice and its flower markets, its Old Town which, like certain parts of Naples, can be visited only on foot, and the very renowned Promenade des Anglais (Walkway of the English) with its endless guard-rail and its chairs all lined up facing the sea; Nice and — the second of its very famous specialties — the entrance in full force of His Majesty King Carnival "into his good city," with a parade of tanks, battles of flowers and confetti, masked processions, ending with the burning of the effigy of this king of an exuberant festival of twelve winter days, on the evening of Mardi Gras (Shrove Tuesday)... Nice and the sound of the waves on its pebbles, Nice and its perfumed hills of Cimiez and Carabacel, Nice and that very special color of its houses built 150 years ago which is called, I believe, *Nice pink*, a compromise between pale ocher and sienna. Here is Nice and its neighbor, almost its suburb, Villefranche, admirable roadstead enclosed by the scintillating sumptuousness of Cape Ferrat.

(Like Picasso at Vallauris for the crypt of the Lérins monks, like Matisse at Vence for the Dominicans' Rosary Chapel, Cocteau took his paint-brush in hand, as a neighbor from Santo-Sospir on Cape Ferrat, to honor the fishermen of Villefranche and conform his mythology to the Gospel illustrations of the simple, naked Saint Peter's Chapel, thus returning to worship — and to paying visitors between services — a long abandoned sanctuary.)

Is this still Provence? Faced with the exemplary whole of this "Great" Riviera which starts at the mouth of the Var and ends at Menton, we are tempted to answer: "Provence, perhaps. Alpes-Maritimes, certainly." Indisputably, from the composition of the sea-side landscape and its background of hills, espaliers, terraces, gardens, mountain ridges, where the cypresses, slender, solitary shafts, count for something, there emanates a sort of Florentine mildness and moderation, an almost Umbrian serenity, which clearly tend to signify that here we have indeed reached the outposts of Italy.

Moreover, here is Beaulieu, and here is Eze-Bord-de-Mer and further along, Cap-d'Ail, from which you can go on foot to Monaco without leaving the coast-line. Here is Beausoleil, steep appendage (in French territory) to Monte-Carlo; here is Roquebrune and its feudal castle, the oldest in France, here is Cape Martin, buried beneath its legendary forests of pine and antique olive-trees.

Here is Menton and its blue mountain, Menton where "winter is indulgent and summer without violence," Menton, the lemon queen, and its giant olive-trees, its churches and their bells, its processions, Menton and its pink roofs, its music festivals, sea-level arrival-point of the triple network of "Corniche" roads, Great, Middle and Lower, starting from Nice; Menton, terminal city...

Because the Romans finally made safe the communication routes between Italy and the Gauls, a monumental ornament was erected at the spot where the triumphal *via* of the Ceasars crossed the barrier of the Alps. This took place in the reign of Augustus, in 5 B.C.; this was the Trophy of La Turbie. The monumental whole reached a height of 165 feet (50 m) with a width of 130 feet (40 m); today there remains only a dismantled ruin, partially reconstructed since 1920, still imposing, however.

There is situated, complement (and completion) of those of the Mount of the May-Tree and the Windmills of Paillas, the third (and last) panoramic meeting-place on this itinerary of the sun spread out over more than 125 miles (200 km), at the place where the French Riviera gets ready to become the Italian Riviera.

You should try to reach it at that ideally propitious hour when the sun, attacking the shore vertically in the rare breeze and the full heat of the beginning of a summer afternoon, dispenses upon the Riviera painting a light which is as glorious as it is eminently favorable... That hour in Provence which should be called the blue hour of the Mediterranean and which often coincides with that of the siesta.

There, over there, is the old Esterel, wild and fabulous, and there, already closer and lower down, the mountain of Eze and its valleys right down to the sea, and then all the sumptuous charms and the vegetal luxuriance of the three-branched isthmus of Cape Ferrat dwarfed amid the waves, the impregnable rocks and shaggy concrete over which extends the sovereignty of the Princes of Monaco, the wooded valley of the Madonna of Laghet, the hair-pin turns on the slopes of Mount Agel and its culminating summit, the somber and heavy projection of Cape Martin, and the background of the Italian coast.

You should try to wait here for night to fall on the mountains, the valleys and the sea, in order to catch, at the moment of supreme remission of the Riviera landscape, the bursting forth of thousands of lights on the somber coast, their wreath-like procession profusely reflected by the nocturnal Mediterranean. Then, you would see something else: when the moon comes up, other scattered lights dancing on the shimmering sea break free from the shore; these are the fishermen's boats leaving for the night. In the distance, to the east, other lights rise in tiers between sky and sea. The loop is looped: it's Italy.

You should watch for the sun's return, on a calm morning in winter or spring, just before this same Provençal coast begins to be transformed into a shore of glory. Then this is what you would notice.

More than anywhere else, the comforts of life prevail there, as witnessed by its sky and its light, the people who live there, the language that's spoken there, but in which can be discerned, in spite of everything, beyond that sky and that light, beyond the profusion of its azure and its colors, the always somewhat tragic serenity which inhabits the Mediterranean shores.

Jacques ROBICHON

TABLE OF ILLUSTRATIONS

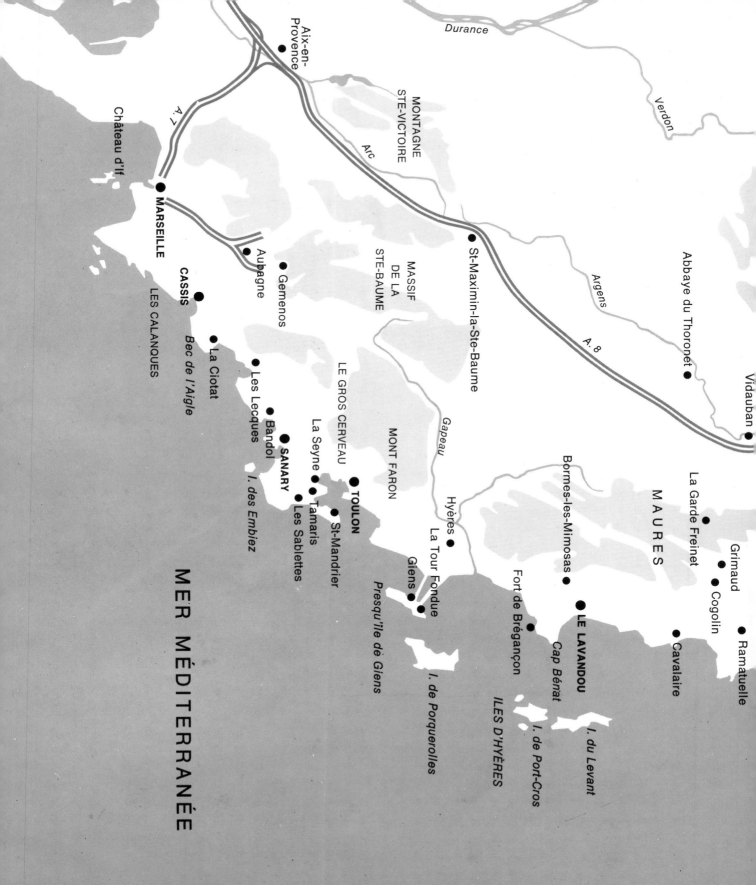

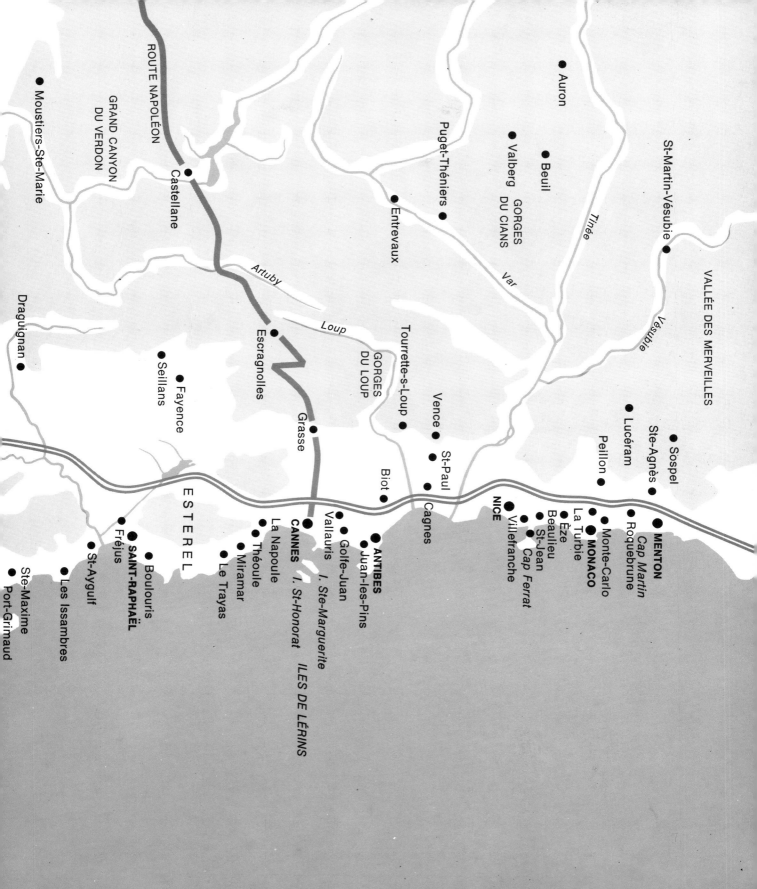

PRINTED JULY 15, 1976 ON THE PRESSES
OF THE FIRMIN-DIDOT PRINTING-HOUSE FOR EDITIONS SUN,
PARIS.

1976 by Editions SUN, PARIS (France)
World Rights Reserved. Printed in France.
ISBN N° 2-7191-0028-5